PRESENTED BY

Patrick Thurman

1994

WESTMINSTER
SCHOOLS

SMYTHE GAMBRELL
LIBRARY

BOOK

Stephen Lee 1993

Conestogas and Stagecoaches

AMERICANS on the Move

Tim McNeese

Crestwood House
New York

Maxwell Macmillan Canada
Toronto

Maxwell Macmillan International
New York Oxford Singapore Sydney

Design and production: Deborah Fillion
Illustrations: © Chris Duke

Crestwood House
Macmillan Publishing Company
866 Third Avenue
New York, NY 10022

Maxwell Macmillan Canada, Inc.
1200 Eglinton Avenue East
Suite 200
Don Mills, Ontario M3C 3N1

Macmillan Publishing Company is part of the
Maxwell Communication Group of Companies.

First edition

Printed in the United States of America

10 9 8 7 6 5 4 3 2 1

Library of Congress Cataloging-in-Publication Data

McNeese, Tim.
     Conestogas and stagecoaches / by Tim McNeese. — 1st ed.
        p. cm. —(Americans on the move)
     Summary: Looks at the role that stagecoaches and Conestoga wagons
played in carrying mail and passengers throughout America, and especially the
West, during the eighteenth and nineteenth centuries.
     ISBN 0-89686-732-3
     1. Coaching—United States—History—Juvenile literature. 2. Wagons—
United States—History—Juvenile literature. [1. Coaching—History. 2. Wagons—
History. 3. Transportation—History.] I. Title. II. Series: McNeese, Tim. Americans
on the move.
HE5747.M38   1993
388.3'228'0973—dc20   91—24064

★

Contents

★

Introduction

No one knows who invented the wheel. But many centuries ago people began using the wheel to help them travel from place to place. Today people use wheels when they ride in cars, buses, taxicabs and trucks. Even giant airplanes land on wheels. The wheel is important to all of us, because it helps us go places.

Early in American history almost everyone owned a wagon. People in cities rode in carriages and coaches. And perhaps the most important wheels that helped move people and goods were those used on stagecoaches and giant Conestoga wagons. Those days of the brightly painted Conestoga wagons and the speedy, adventurous trips people made in stage-coaches along the early American roads were exciting for both drivers and passengers alike.

Americans Move West

Over 200 years ago the United States stretched only from the Atlantic Ocean west to the Mississippi River. Beyond the Mississippi the country had not been settled. As the country grew bigger over the years, Americans looked for faster ways to travel longer distances. Many pioneers and settlers wanted to move west, but just traveling from state to state was hard enough to do.

In the early 1800s many settlers were moving west of the Ohio River. People needed better roads to help them get to the western part of the country.

In 1811 Americans began building a new road from the East to the West. Men built the new road from Cumberland, Maryland, to Wheeling, Virginia (now West Virginia). The government spent $7 million making the road. It was first called the Great National Pike but later was called the **National Road**. Two important ways of traveling on the National Road were by the Conestoga wagon and the early stagecoach.

The National Road was built to help early American
settlers move from the eastern states to the West.

Conestoga Wagons

Early in America's history Americans who tried to take wagons across the eastern mountains called the Appalachians found the job very difficult. Most wagons could not stand the rough trips up and down steep hills and mountains. The Conestoga wagon was the first wagon in America that could go just about anyplace.

Wagons like the Conestoga were probably first used in the countries of Germany and England. But the real Conestogas were built in Pennsylvania by a group of people called the **Pennsylvania Dutch**. These people had come from Germany and many of them lived together in Lancaster County, about 60 miles west of Philadelphia. The Pennsylvania Dutch living in the Conestoga Valley made the wagons we know as Conestogas.

The Pennsylvania Dutch in Lancaster County had large farms. The farmers grew lots of grain and vegetables and raised big herds of hogs, cattle, sheep and horses. They cut down trees and made lumber.

Other people living along the **frontier**, away from the cities, had things they needed to have taken to the cities and towns to sell. Trappers had furs. Millers had flour. Blacksmiths had iron products. Many people needed a wagon that could haul a large amount over long distances. The Conestoga wagon was just what people needed. The trip from Lancaster to Philadelphia took four days on a bad road. People needed a strong wagon that would not fall apart and could carry a heavy load.

The first mention of the "Conestoga wagon" was in 1717. The early Conestogas were used to carry furs from Lancaster to Philadelphia. Later the wagons were used to haul farm goods. They were even used to carry things like bears' oil and honey. The Conestogas soon became the most popular wagon for carrying lots of heavy goods to market. They were very well made by the best wagon makers in America.

By 1800 Conestoga wagons were being used all over the United States. When the National Road was built, these wagons traveled the road from one end to the other. In just a few years at least 5,000 Conestoga wagons were being used on the National Road, hauling everything people needed to live along the frontier.

Wagons Built to Last

The men who built Conestoga wagons made them very carefully. They made their wagons so they would be very strong and last a long time. Wagon makers also wanted to make the Conestoga a beautiful wagon.

The Conestoga wagon had a curved bottom. Both ends of the wagon tilted up to keep things from

*Early Conestoga wagons were well built
to carry heavy loads over long distances.*

falling out when the wagon went up and down hills. The wagon bed was about three feet deep, ten feet long and 3½ feet wide. There was no seat on the front of the wagon. The man driving the wagon often walked along beside the wagon or rode one of the horses. Great wood bows looped over the top of the wagon. A big white canvas covered the wagon to protect the goods inside from the rain. The canvas cover could be closed on each end. Some wagons had only eight bows, while some had as many as 16.

Most wagons had a toolbox on the left side of the wagon bed. Often the hinges of the toolbox were shaped like flowers, snakes or hearts. The feed trough for the horses was chained to the back of the wagon. A metal holder was put on the side of the wagon bed. This metal piece held an ax.

Most Conestoga wagon beds were painted bright blue. The wheels were painted deep red. The wheels were large and wooden, often at least four inches wide. This was because wagons with wide wheels were easier to pull than wagons with narrow wheels. Most Conestoga wheels were about 60 inches apart. The back wheels were bigger than the front wheels.

Conestoga wagon wheels were considered works of art. They were carefully made by the best wheel makers, called **wheelwrights**. The wheels on a Conestoga were very important. Since the wheels were the part of the wagon to touch the bumpy roads, a wagon was only as good as its wheels.

Special Horses for a Special Job

For all the care and beauty that went into making a Conestoga wagon, the horses that pulled the big wagons were just as beautiful. In fact the type of horse used was a breed called Conestoga which does not exist today. But they were special horses that were used for a special purpose—pulling Conestoga wagons.

The Conestoga wagon was big and heavy when loaded with freight, so powerful horses were required. These horses had strong legs and bodies. They were also very tame animals. Most Conestoga horses were black or reddish brown. They stood over 16 hands high (that's how horses are measured) and weighed about 1,650 pounds.

The men who drove Conestoga wagons took good care of their horses. They matched their horses by color and decorated the horses' harnesses with special bells. These bells made a merry, jingling noise as a Conestoga went along the road. Some wagoners put other decorations on their horses, like **pom-poms**, to make their horses more noticeable to people.

Teamsters Drive the Wagons

All the men who drove the big Conestoga wagons were called **teamsters**. Those who drove the wagons for a living were regulars. Others who drove the wagons only during certain parts of the year were called **militia men**. Regular teamsters looked down on those men who drove wagons only part-time.

Hitching up a team of horses to a Conestoga was a difficult job. Most wagons were pulled by four, five or six horses. It would take a good teamster to keep all the harnesses, leather straps and collars straight as he put his horses on his wagon each morning. The horses always knew that work was ahead when they were getting hitched. They waited patiently for the word that would tell them it was time to begin a new day. At last the teamster was ready to go. Only then would he give his horses a loud "Giddap!" and the day of traveling would begin.

When a teamster chose to ride a horse, it was the horse closest to the wagon on the left. The teamster would have a special saddle on that horse. That horse was called the **wheelhorse**.

The teamster held a piece of leather called a **jerk line.** He used this line to guide his horses. The other end of the jerk line was tied to a bit in the left front horse's mouth. This long leather strap was the teamster's only tie to the horses. Good teamsters did not even have to use their jerk lines. They could often shout to the horses to go, turn or stop. The horses knew just what the teamster wanted.

From 1820 to 1850 Conestoga wagons carried most of the goods hauled by road. These wagons could carry a lot of weight. Because the wagons were so big and heavy, they traveled only about two miles an hour. Most wagons moved only about 12 to 15 miles a day.

The men who drove Conestoga wagons were much like our truck drivers today. Wagoners had the important job of seeing that what the merchandise people needed was carried across the early American roads from town to town. Conestoga wagon drivers were hard workers. Their days were busy with the difficult roads, strong horses and other traffic, such as stagecoaches and small carts.

Life on the Road

Teamsters often traveled together in long lines of wagons. Each morning the teamsters would start early. They would hurry through breakfast and then get their wagon trains together for the day's trip. They would stop for an hour or two at noon at a wagon **tavern** stop. Everyone could rest, especially the horses.

★

*Conestoga horses were special animals
that were well cared for by their drivers.*

★

Everyone would eat, too. The animals would get their feed. Because of all the hard work they had done, the men would eat lots of food. Sometimes they would meet friends and other wagoners going the other direction along the roads. After eating and resting the wagoners would start up again.

Conestoga wagon tavern stops, or stands, were found all along the major wagon roads. Many of the stands looked alike. They were usually square buildings made of stone. They had two stories and an attic with windows at each end. Usually a porch stretched across the front of the building. There were two doors to the stand. One door went to a room where the teamsters could go to drink and talk together. The other door led to a hall and the tavern keeper's rooms.

The teamsters met in a room that was about 18 by 30 feet. This may sound large, but when the room was full of dozens of wagoners, it was small indeed! There was always a fire in a huge fireplace to warm the teamsters during the winter months. There was nothing like a roaring, cheery fire to make the teamsters feel good at the end of a long, cold day of traveling.

Evening at the Stands

Stagecoach travelers and Conestoga wagon drivers did not usually stay at the same taverns on the main roads, like the National Road. At wagon taverns a wagoner would put his horses in the wagon yard. The horses would be left outside for the night, even if it rained. On very cold nights wagoners would cover the horses with blankets.

Horses were tied to the wagon tongue, with three horses on each side. The tongue is the harnessing pole attached to the front of the wagon. They ate out of the feed trough, which was carried on the back of the

Teamsters often stopped at tavern stands along the road to relax and enjoy themselves after a hard day's work.

★

wagon. The feed trough was attached to the tongue when the horses were feeding. A watering trough stood in the inn yard. There was a big pasture where the horses could munch the grass. Nearby was a barn loaded with hay during the winter.

Teamsters would usually pay about 12½ cents. A drink of whiskey was three cents. If a wagoner ordered two drinks at the same time, he paid only five cents for both of them.

The wagoners slept on the tavern floor on their own blankets. Often before going to sleep, the wagoners would stay up drinking, singing and dancing. Sometimes they would play jokes and tricks on one another. A fiddle would sometimes provide the music for dancing. The men would dance jigs, hoedowns and reels. As many as two or three dozen men might dance at the same time.

They were like a bunch of grizzly bears, all having fun. Finally, when it was late, the men would begin to unroll their bedding and lay them out on the floor. If the weather was cold they would all lie with their feet toward the warm tavern fire. Soon the snoring of all these big men would fill the tavern.

Changes in the Western Wagon

As more and more Americans in the 1840s and 1850s moved west of the Mississippi River, so did the Conestoga wagon. The wagon was put to new uses in the West since the land was different from the East. So the new "western wagons" began to look different from the old Conestogas.

With the western Conestogas oxen were used instead of horses and mules. The oxen were cheaper for western freight companies to use. Also, Indians would not steal oxen as they would horses. Oxen would eat prairie grass and did not need special feed as horses often did.

The running gear on the wagons was also changed, so the wagons could make sharper turns. The raised ends of the wagons were changed to an upright position. A seat was added to the front of the wagon.

The wagons began to grow in size. Nearly all western Conestogas had iron tires four inches wide and could carry 7,000 pounds of goods and supplies. Western freight men sometimes hitched one wagon to another, in much the same way as our modern big-rig trucks pull two trailers.

Trading on the Santa Fe Trail

Just as in the East, wagons out West were used to haul goods and freight. Freight wagons on the Santa Fe Trail looked very much like the Conestogas. The Santa Fe Trail ran from Missouri to what is today Santa Fe, New Mexico. At that time Santa Fe was part of the country of Mexico. American traders and merchants began trading along the trail after Mexico gained its independence from Spain in 1821. Freight wagon trains on the Santa Fe Trail often covered ten to fifteen miles a day. At night the freight wagons would be put into a square. The oxen, horses and mules would be put inside this "wagon corral." The corral of wagons also served as protection against Indian attacks.

The trip from Missouri to New Mexico usually took from two to three months. The Santa Fe Trail was about 800 miles long. Once the American wagon train, loaded with everything from whiskey to pianos, entered the Mexican town of Santa Fe, many people would stream out into the street to watch the wagons coming into town. The traders would be dressed in their "Sunday suits" and would often show off for the local people by seeing who could crack his whip the loudest.

★

The Santa Fe trail was one of the longest trade routes in the United States during the days of the wagon.

★

Wagon Trails West

By the 1850s most wagons made in America were made by three companies. The Pitt Company in Pittsburgh, Pennsylvania, made wagons that looked very much like Conestogas. The other two companies—one in St. Louis, the other in Indiana—made wagons to use on farms. These wagons could each carry about 5,000 pounds. Sometimes these two companies also made freight wagons, like the Conestogas.

Many long wagon roads became important in the West. These roads carried many Americans across thousands of miles to California and Oregon. To get to these places, western travelers went along the Oregon and California trails. New wagons, which were very different from the Conestogas, were developed to carry people and their household goods. These wagons were smaller and lighter than Conestogas. Conestogas were rarely used to carry people west of the Mississippi River.

Wagons Supplying Army Posts

Wagons like the Conestogas were used in the 1850s to supply army posts and forts out West. Several freight companies were paid to deliver goods such as guns, clothing and barrels of pork, salt and cornmeal to the western forts. One of the biggest companies was Russell, Majors and Waddell.

This company spent half a million dollars buying 3,500 oxen and 500 wagons. These wagons were divided into 20 wagon trains, each made up of 25 wagons. Russell, Majors and Waddell agreed to supply the army with 2½ million pounds of supplies.

These freight wagon trains were carefully packed. Each wagon was pulled by 12 oxen. Between 20 and 30 extra oxen were taken along. Each freight wagon train had its own wagon master, his helper and a teamster for each wagon. Another man was also hired to watch over the extra oxen. Two or three other men went along with the wagon train, in case of sickness or death of any teamsters.

Once a Russell, Majors and Waddell freight wagon train was on its way, the wagons usually covered about 15 miles a day. The teamsters took a long break at noon to rest themselves and their oxen. Sometimes a freight wagon train traveled at night because the days were hot.

Wagon freighting was important until the 1880s. As railroads stretched across the West, freight wagon use dropped off. They were used only in areas where trains did not run. More and more freight wagons were used to carry supplies over short distances, from town to town, instead of on long routes.

Stagecoaches

The first long stagecoach line in the United States began in 1785. It ran north from New York City to Albany, the state capital. But stagecoach travel was very difficult at that time.

The early stagecoaches used in America were built in England. These English stagecoaches were very heavy and large. They were not made for American roads. American roads were very bumpy and full of holes. English stagecoaches bounced passengers on metal springs. Sometimes the English stagecoaches would turn over when they went around corners too fast. People in America soon began looking for a way to make better stagecoaches.

By the 1770s carriage makers in the New England states began building egg-shaped stagecoaches. These coaches were lighter and smaller than the English coaches and they did not tip over as easily. The springs were also taken out. American coach makers put the coach bodies on heavy leather straps. This made the

The egg-shaped stagecoaches of the 1770s were safer and more comfortable to ride than the older English models.

ride smoother. Soon, riding on a new American stage-coach was more like floating instead of bumping.

But the new stagecoaches had problems too. People could not stand up in the egg-shaped coaches without hitting their heads. The seats inside the stage-coach were narrow. The egg-shaped coaches could not carry any baggage on top.

A New Kind of Stagecoach

In 1813 a man named Lewis Downing opened a little wagon shop in Concord, New Hampshire where he built stagecoaches. He had a young helper named Stephen Abbot who changed the way stagecoaches were made.

Abbot made them lighter and he made the wheels stronger. He also changed the shape so that baggage could go on top of the coaches. His new stagecoaches were soon called Concord coaches. The Concord coach was such a good stagecoach that soon every stage driver in the United States wanted one.

Concord coaches were bought for use in other countries around the world, from England to Australia. Over the years Downing and Abbot made many changes on their Concord coaches to make them even better. Soon stagecoaches could be found everywhere. Every big city and almost every little village had regular stagecoach service.

Stagecoach Craftsmanship

These new coaches were much more comfortable than earlier stagecoaches. On each side there was a door with a glass window that opened. There were other windows to let in the sunlight. Leather curtains covered the windows to keep out the cold weather.

★

Concord stagecoaches earned worldwide
popularity in the early 1800s.

★

Concord coaches were painted many times and covered with **varnish**. This gave the coaches smooth, hard surfaces. The coaches were polished until they shone like a mirror. The coach body was usually painted red and an artist would paint a picture on each door. The wood inside the coach was very fancy. The name of the person or company buying the coach was often written in gold paint above the doors. The steps and railing on top of the coach were painted black while the coach's brakes and gears were painted yellow. Small red lines were painted on the wheel spokes for decoration. Two big square brass candle lamps were put on the front of the coach for lights.

Most American stagecoaches had three seats, and each seat held three passengers. People in the front seat sat with their backs to the driver. The people in the other two seats faced the horses. A tenth rider could sit on the outside seat with the driver. When it

Abbot and Downing built two kinds of coaches that were less expensive than the Concord: the celerity wagon and the mud wagon.

was a nice day, most people liked sitting there instead of inside the coach. But a rider could sit next to the stagecoach driver only when invited. Sometimes important people, such as judges and senators, were invited to sit with the driver. And occasionally the driver would ask a pretty lady to sit by him to enjoy the sunny day.

Passengers could put their baggage under their seats or in a place in the rear of the stage called a boot. Soon stagecoaches were built with flat roofs so people could put their baggage on top of the coach and out of the way. This change also made for more room inside the coach.

Different Kinds of Coaches

The light Concord stagecoach weighed approximately 2,500 pounds. It sold for about $1,200, which was considered a lot of money at that time. These coaches were too expensive for many stage companies. Abbot and Downing built two kinds of cheaper coaches. They were called mud wagons and celerity wagons. Celerity is a word meaning fast. These coaches were not as fancy as Concord coaches, but they were just as strong and well made.

Mud wagons were made for use in deep mud and on very rough roads. Celerity wagons were made for quick delivery of the mail. Both of these coaches were small and light. They could carry six average-sized passengers. The coaches had no doors or windows. Instead they had open sides. In bad weather the openings were covered by canvas curtains that were rolled down. The coach roofs were also made of canvas. The two coaches were very much alike, although mud wagons were made extra strong and celerity wagons were made very light. Each coach cost about $500.

Traveling by Stagecoach

Stagecoaches were the cheapest way to travel long distances. It sometimes cost as little as three dollars to travel 100 miles. In addition a passenger usually paid one dollar to sleep at a stage tavern. He or she would pay about 25 cents for dinner.

Stagecoach trips began early in the day. Most drivers started at three or four in the morning. The driver gave his passengers half an hour to stumble from their beds into the coach. The waiting horses pawed at the ground, ready to get away.

Once the stagecoach was on the road, the first three or four stops were only to change horses. After four or five hours on the road, the coach reached a tavern. Only then would the travelers get their first cup of coffee and breakfast.

Changing Horses

Because the National Road was such a good road, many people used it. There were always lots of stagecoaches and wagons on the road. On many days a dozen or more stagecoaches would leave Wheeling at the same time. They were all traveling to the same place. Sometimes these stagecoaches would race one another. Soon they would come to the next station along the road, where the tired horses would be changed for fresh ones. People at the stations would change the horses in less than a minute. Sometimes the horses were changed so fast that fresh horses were ready to go before the coach had even stopped rocking!

Most stagecoaches could be driven from Wheeling to Cumberland in 24 hours. The distance between these two towns is 130 miles. Usually stagecoaches would travel between five and six miles an hour.

Stopping at Taverns

Every 40 or 50 miles along a stage route, the coach came to a tavern. Here hungry passengers could eat. Most taverns looked about the same. There was a long porch along the front. The outside walls were covered with **handbills** and newspapers. Frequently the taverns were not very clean inside. Tables were covered with big brown canvas tablecloths. They were usually dirty and not washed very often. Food was served on tin plates.

There was plenty of food, though. Passengers might eat meat, chicken, fish, sausages, eggs and dried beans, all at the same meal. The meal was served when the stage driver sat down. When he finished and was ready to go, the meal was over. The passengers had to get up and leave even if they wanted more to eat!

Stagecoach travelers usually spent their
nights in dirty, overcrowded taverns.

The tavern keepers served food when they were ready. If a stagecoach arrived after a meal had been served, its passengers had to wait until the next meal. Dinner was served in the middle of the day. Supper, however, was usually at the end of the stage-riding day. The traveler ate where he or she was going to sleep. Eating at a tavern was called having a public dinner.

Sleeping on the Road

Sleeping in a tavern was not a very pleasant experience. Stage drivers carried their own bedding. They usually spread it out on the floor after the other travelers had gone upstairs to their beds. A driver's favorite place to sleep was under the tavern table. There, he would not get stepped on in the night. A stagecoach driver paid 75 cents a night to sleep in the tavern and to have his horses fed.

Travelers paid one dollar for a bed upstairs. Often there were only two rooms—one for men and one for women. A large tavern had more rooms, but sometimes there were five or six beds in each one. Strangers shared rooms. They even had to share beds. The beds were covered with dirty brown sheets. Many tavern beds had bedbugs. And there was always someone who snored loudly, keeping the passengers awake. Some people chose to sleep out in the barn.

Delivering the Mail

Concord coaches were made to carry the United States mail, as well as people. Mail coaches could often be seen along the National Road. They had gold-painted sides, with a picture on each side of a postboy sitting on a flying horse, blowing his horn.

Inside, nine passengers sat on plush silk cushions. Riding the mail coach was a special treat.

A mail coach passenger bought a ticket for every 100 pounds of weight. A passenger who weighed 200 pounds or more had to buy two tickets. Each person could take only 15 pounds of baggage because the mailbags took up so much space. Mail coach drivers had orders to treat their passengers with courtesy. But they did not have to be at all polite to slow drivers. Anyone driving a wagon or cart who got in the way of a stage driver could be arrested.

The Men Who Drove the Stages

Stagecoach drivers were very important people. Many thought a driver's work was an exciting adventure. Some of the best drivers became famous because they drove very fast.

Luxurious mail coaches could often be seen along the National Road.

Homer Westover was a famous stagecoach driver. People along the National Road knew he was one of the best drivers. He once set a speed record by driving his stagecoach over ten miles in 45 minutes. Westover was driving very fast that day because he was delivering a special message addressed to Congress by President Martin Van Buren. On the same trip Westover drove his stagecoach from Frederick, Maryland, to Wheeling—about 222 miles—in 23½ hours. He had to drive his stagecoach about ten miles an hour, which was very fast for a stagecoach.

Redding Bunting was another famous stage-coach driver. He was very tall and stood very straight. He had large, strong hands, a red face and a big, booming voice. Bunting drove a Concord mail coach that was pulled by six matching horses. His most famous drive was to deliver a message from President James K. Polk that a war was starting between the United States and

★

The best stagecoach drivers and coaches were
always chosen to deliver important messages.

Mexico. Bunting drove 131 miles in 12 hours. That was a speed of nearly 11 miles an hour! His passengers that day said they would never forget that ride!

There were many stagecoach companies. Some of them had funny names such as the June Bug Line, the Oyster Line and the Shake Gut Line. The Oyster Line was famous for delivering oysters to people out West. Stagecoaches on the Shake Gut Line drove very fast to deliver packages of food that might spoil.

Special People, Special Trips

Every year the most exciting event on the stagecoach lines was the delivery of the president's annual message to Congress. People out West wanted to hear what the president had to say. So stagecoach companies chose their best drivers and told them to drive as fast as possible to carry the message to the people. Driving ten miles an hour, the coaches sometimes covered 150 or 200 miles. All along the road, people lined up to watch these fast stagecoaches and cheer the drivers on. Travelers did not like to ride with these special coaches because they went too fast. People knew they would have an exciting but very bumpy ride.

Sometimes the president of the United States would travel by stagecoach on the National Road. When he did, the stagecoach company he chose built a new coach just for him. Or the company would use its best stagecoach. These stagecoaches were specially painted. The coach was named for the president. An artist would paint the president's name or nickname on the door in bright red or blue. Such a stagecoach might be named General Jackson or The President. Only the best drivers got to drive a president's special stagecoach. Some drivers became famous because they had driven a stagecoach that carried the president.

★

When the California gold rush began, the need for
stagecoach service and skilled drivers increased.

Taking the Stage
to the West

The first stagecoach line west of the Missouri River was in Oregon. Called the **Telegraph Line**, this regular stage service was started in 1846. With the discovery of gold in California in 1848, stagecoaches were soon moving across the Far West.

In the fall of 1849 John Whistman began a stage line between San Francisco in northern California and San Jose in the South, along the major road called *El Camino Real*. In the Spanish language that means The Royal Highway.

Many of the men who drove the early California stagecoaches were those who had lost their jobs in the East when railroads began to replace stages. Several of these men had gone to Mexico to drive stagecoaches, even before gold was discovered in California. When the gold rush began, these former eastern stage drivers were eager to go north to California.

★

As more and more people moved to California to work in the gold camps, the need for regular stagecoach service across the West increased. Demands for a mail service from the eastern states to the Pacific Coast grew until 1857. In that year the U.S. Congress began support for an overland mail service. The government wanted someone to establish stagecoach service across the West so that a traveler could get from Missouri to California in less than 25 days.

Butterfield Overland Mail

The first stagecoach company to build a line from the eastern states to California was called the Overland Mail Company. (Many people called it the Butterfield Overland Mail, after John Butterfield, the company's president.)

This first overland route went across the Southwest Territories (today's Texas, New Mexico and Arizona). The journey was nearly 2,800 miles long. Most of the trip was across a wilderness populated by Indians. Part of the trip also had to be made through the desert.

To get the stage line started, Butterfield bought 1,000 horses, 500 mules and 500 coaches. Most of the coaches were Concord celeritys. Butterfield spent over $1 million for all the livestock and coaches. He hired 800 men to keep the line going. These men drove the stages, lived at stops along the route and cared for the horses and mules. By September 1858 the Butterfield Overland Mail Line was open for business.

The first man to travel all the way across the new route was Waterman Ormsby, a newspaperman. The trip took him 23 days, 23 hours and 30 minutes from St. Louis to San Francisco. He arrived in San Francisco on October 9, 1858. At last one could travel by stagecoach from the eastern United States all the way to California!

★

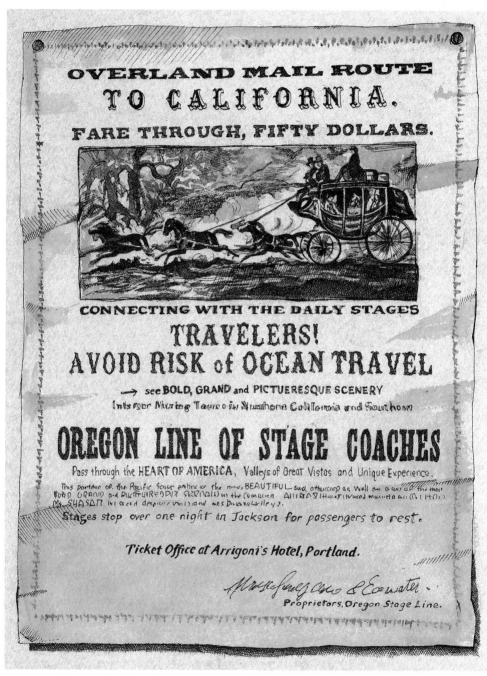

The Overland Mail Company was the first stagecoach company to build a line from the eastern states to California. ★

Travelers on the Overland Route had to pass through wilderness and desert areas on their 2,800 mile journey to California.

★

Western Stage Travel

Stagecoach travel across the West was not easy. The stages rolled along, day and night, for over three weeks per trip. Passengers found it hard to sleep. The western stage line did not have nice tavern stations for its passengers. Stations along the route, usually about ten to fifteen miles apart, often offered little comfort. Travelers complained about bad food and the fact that the stations did not have good toilets. Also, passengers could not bathe. Some people thought that a number of the stage drivers drank too much. Add the dust of the hot, dry Southwest, and people found "stageing" across the country very unpleasant.

Stages in Colorado

When gold was discovered in Colorado, around the mountain called Pikes Peak, a stagecoach line was started. William H. Russell, an important western businessman who owned a company that hauled goods by wagon to the western towns and mining camps, organized the Leavenworth and Pike's Peak Express Company.

To get the stagecoach line started, Russell and a partner named John S. Jones hired 108 men to live at stagecoach stations along the 680-mile route. The two men bought 800 mules and 50 new Concord stagecoaches from the Abbot-Downing Company of New Hampshire. The new stagecoach line began daily service between Leavenworth, Kansas, and Denver, Colorado, on April 18, 1850. Miners and prospectors looking for gold and silver could now travel to the "diggings" in a stagecoach.

End of the Line

Stageing had come to the West and eventually became an important way to travel. For over 50 years stages continued to service western towns, both large and small, long after the West was settled. Some stages

The era of the stagecoach and the Conestoga wagon was an exciting and adventurous period in American transportation history.

continued after 1900. For several decades in this century, a western traveler could take a stagecoach to lots of out-of-the-way places.

The old Abbot-Downing Company, which built the first Concord stagecoaches, began to become less important as horse-drawn vehicles were replaced by cars and trucks. By the turn of the century Abbot-Downing made very few stagecoaches. Instead the company made horse-drawn ambulances, circus wagons and cannon carriages. Later Abbot-Downing made truck bodies and fire engines.

By 1920 the Abbot-Downing Company had stopped making vehicles. It was simply too expensive for the company's skilled craftsmen and artisans to make cars and trucks. By that time nearly all vehicles made in the United States were mass-produced in big factories.

★

Dreaming of Days Gone By

Both the Conestoga wagons and the stagecoaches of early America were very important. They helped to move people from place to place. They carried goods over long distances to the cities. Life on the frontier was made easier by these two kinds of "wheels."

There are not very many Conestoga wagons or stagecoaches left today. They were no longer important once the railroads were built. Trains were able to move more goods and more people than wagons and coaches.

Conestogas and stagecoaches may still be seen in museums and at historical places. These mighty wheeled vehicles remind today's travelers of the difficulties people had in traveling 150 years ago, when speeding stagecoaches raised dust along America's early roads and Conestogas carried goods to market with their horses' bells jingling.

For Further Reading

Earle, Alice. *Stagecoach and Tavern Days*. Salem: Aver Co. Publishers, 1970.

Holmes, Oliver. *Stagecoach East*. Washington, D. C.: Smithsonian, 1983.

Stein, Conrad. *The Story of the Pony Express*. Chicago: Children's Press, 1981.

Tunis, Edwin. *Wheels: A Pictorial History*. New York: Harper Collins Children's Books, 1977.

Glossary

El Camino Real —Spanish name meaning "The Royal Highway."

frontier—Region marking the end of settlement.

handbill—A small, printed sheet or pamphlet given to people by hand.

jerk line—Leather line used by a teamster to guide a Conestoga wagon's horses.

militia man—A man who drove a Conestoga wagon as part-time work during certain times of the year.

National Road—Begun in 1811, it was a government-built road running from Cumberland, Maryland, to Vandalia, Illinois. For decades it was the best road to use in traveling west to the Mississippi.

Pennsylvania Dutch—German immigrants who settled in the farming lands of Pennsylvania. Many of them lived in Lancaster, Pennsylvania.

★

pom-pom—An ornamental ball used for decoration.

tavern—A roadside inn where travelers could usually eat, drink and sleep.

teamster—A man who drove a Conestoga wagon.

Telegraph Line—Located in Oregon, it was the first stagecoach line west of the Missouri River.

varnish—A liquid that, when brushed on a surface, dries to a shiny, protective finish.

wheelhorse—The horse located closest to a Conestoga wagon's left wheel. Sometimes a teamster rode on this horse.

wheelwright—A person who makes and repairs wheels.

Index